Lightsheen

(Subsea sheen)

poems by

Alexandra Gilliam

Finishing Line Press
Georgetown, Kentucky

Lightsheen

(Subsea sheen)

ACKNOWLEDGMENTS

Birds, Night Breech, and Crawlspace
have appeared in chapbook Femmestuary, dancing girl press

Rio de Janero, Texas Yellow Jacket, and *Crawlspace III* have appeared on
Aspasiology in response to Donna de la Perrière's poetry.

Slang , Migrantlight, and *gOD's Ear* have appeared in Second Stutter Volume
2.

Exile VIII and *Graffiti* have appeared in LIT No. 30 Winter 2017.

Exile II, III, IV and *Crawlspace I, II* have appeared in In Parentheses
Magazine.

Publisher: Leah Maines
Editor: Christen Kincaid
Cover Art: Alexandra Gilliam
Author Photo: Alexandra Gilliam
Cover Design: Elizabeth Maines McCleavy

Order online: www.finishinglinepress.com
also available on amazon.com

Author inquiries and mail orders:
Finishing Line Press
P. O. Box 1626
Georgetown, Kentucky 40324
U. S. A.

Table of Contents

For Constance & Clélie —

In memory of Hunter Deely--

you are always here & on the beginning of a thought

"Perhaps home is not a place but simply an irrevocable condition."

James Baldwin, *Giovanni's Room*

"the spirits have abandoned me; let me not abandon myself—"

Brenda Hillman, *Seasonal Works with Letters on Fire*

BIRDS

I am putting shells on sand
I am hiding shells beneath the surface
I am sinning shells to sand
singing dust to the surface
singing specs of nothingness out of the sand
binding little leaflets
hot gluing specs of white shell backs
holding flecks and letting them slide
I am painting the ground to existence
I pour my lip on the ground
folding, beating, covering existence
steaming, baking, frying existence
Imagine this: hanging earrings through your existence
clatter of birds through paint
I am undressing the sand
pouring each sand crease, each toe print
ballooning jellyfish
hanging black suit on a rusty nail
hanging mother's robe on a busted pendant
hanging books upside the shore
dancing space between my fingers
I am slim lights
I want to sleep your eyes: the burning dusk, the leaping dusk,
            the binding dusk, birds of America I want to sleep your eyes

NIGHT BREECH

Love chips hooked to my leg
your night; your face

Night a series of blank oceans
persimmon pressed nape

And neck
And kiss

Fish kissing bone
conjure lips
your night; your face

Anyone's night
my dark spilling dark
spilling your face

The ocean
The spill

The bodies
pressing back

CRAWLSPACE

Nothing will ever
be this simple, this elegant
steeple out
on a lip, snatched
up, moving through
edge of street
 grass burn
sweet, wring toes out
window, press
nails to air
vent, mud
son, he said, this is simple
crack of match
high on
river
bend the paper towards
the mouth
don't breathe just
fly

CITYSCAPE #6

He told me the government pulled the plug and they
blasted the sweet lipped Ka-tri- na levees to kingdom come
then all that water was straight up past that light post he
uses his hand lifts it as high as he can over his head almost
reaching on the balls of his feet and I wish I could have been
there to feel my body fall limp as in rising water

CITYSCAPE # 9

A tree in the marsh

    Milk box kids

        Car jam
    Milk crate
        Water rising
Freeway

Gun ring
    Freeway

Two tires
    One bottle
No cans
No crates
        Gun down
Freeway

City
    fall open like mouths
    unhinged screen doors

sing me dizzy

CITYSCAPE #27

The girls on the doorstep muddying the doormat the girls
holding girls without their fathers hands girls with orange
scented skin like bar soap little orange blossoms in an empty
soccer field girls with lit papers pinched between their fingers
girls in tattered nightgowns girls with shells in their jean
pockets the girls heavy eyelids the girls trashcan girls pale
pink and painted hearts and flowers like sunny side up
breakfasts like vagabonds like trespassers

CRAWLSPACE

forget what you know—levee breath—pavement fallen-—
drowning eye—water rip glass—I am sinking your hand—
swallowing hymns— hang it in the middle —pull sound out of
the kitchen—bundle roof over your shoulder—make shift
religion—rattle coins down the hallway— water high

CRAWLSPACE

tell me how you really feel—blue—no wet bones—no bird
song—handful of sun—hold my foot against the pavement—
white flowers embroidered flag—to overflow—to go daughter
in the head— mirror high— wave like cool—swollen from
water —spellbound—jazz on skillet—magnolia right after it
opens—rain on a pedal—call me bathroom graffiti—catch
air—snow milk—make a lake your hands— to go to her—
speak

CRAWLSPACE

Drown; permeate; underwater rug;

a hugging Jesus; push that strand behind your ear and sit up starlight;

it's glory on your toes; don't sleep next to that light in myself;

watching the news, waiting, waiting, waiting; her bike

floating in a river; an inevitability that you are watching;

      burn my dress off my body;

      this body wants it all

he keeps saying you smell so nice; head under river;

swarm of bees; lava lamp of despair;

sing termites scream;

you want to believe

SLANG

Let sound
beat doves let frozen
beat doves let humidity and slips and orange
beat doves let shadow
beat dove let parallel honey mind
beat doves let peach flu
beat doves let breeze stain
palm gospel and
to-go coffee
to death let sound
spigot let clouds
snatch windblown seed let young
let young sound breathe dust
uproot the inner ear sprinkle conch let sound
have
tender fur against skin
hear foot prints
on paint

SINGLESPEED

white sky
                walk silt
man living
        in his car
                single
speed running
        out of
lip spell
bound tumbling
pieces
         over self
trying not
                to slip

EXILE

This isn't a letter
poverty like swimming, the lake crash,
women blinking—

What's your favorite part of history?
sinking your toes in paint,
hook pull you from the ground, pour
water through your legs,
      I am melted lights

EXILE

Cockfight, nails singing sand   just art burning air—

I–only-need-to-feed-my-child-god-stop

Dream me up and spit me out this new head

Bones

something like unraveling

EXILE

mattress between two bodies

Exhaust   broken down speech

underwear pinched
between toes

lull Y2K
lull yarn
lull yards
lull young
lull yes

lull it all back
          underground

EXILE

be hair, cup up,
your mouth,
eyes, burning on water,
sweets, sweet water,

bodies,
bodies lipped water

bodies out your mouth

lip on god's back

Be island
Be glass
Be a man with his hands up

EXILE

Be rose
Be father
Be another world

Dream
domino

EXILE

    be pink, be earthquake, be night,

        be next best thing

    Children all rolled up in a sleeve

Her everything

EXILE

I can't breathe, it's swamp all over my eyelids,

it's mother's eyes, hair all over,

it's light, light bleeding,

bleeding out on water,

it's water, water spooning night,

shaped like bodies,
                    bodies pooling

gOD'S EAR

I wanted your sleep; the writing that took you; to see your
hands; rolled sleeves; the melted porch in grey downpour;
the light in skin; humidity; your grey soft; we felt it seep
through the floor; humidity so calm; fog bleed paper; you
slept at the table; wetness leaned over us; clipped from grey
sky; breathing; your face; wetness a dark rim; burned; grey
slipped up your arm; saw sleep; our betweens; opened you
up; your face; your tired love soaking holes; you are faded;
afraid; my language falling; I comforted him; brought love
down the stairs; held your upper arm; blue in light; morning
going up; coming down

GRAFFITI

dream talk bat eyes

mother like fire fragile

hold face time in your palm

cup sun spot

eye tide lull black

down her face

RIO DE JANEIRO

women reduced to this notion
watermelon by the beach
surreal enough for the moon

The dream catcher your dad gave you as a token

leave this patch

Dream washed over

boy sleeping over your head
a box of needles under
sold his head for a gold match

put your hands together

women will be will be

EXILE

I know this is going
        to be painful

      fit of night

hold your head
still, make
your children
           run
 bring the
      furniture out

        wet pressed
        to cloth

night across
      your face

always more
         inside than
         air

     it's this side
     of the south
         hanging
    out of
the river
     stay

     till home
     sins

hook objects

        out eye

   silver fish
   wet carpet
   silver head to floor

commit it
to sighs

the night
just holds

DEPENDENCY

angel, star athlete, heart ache,
won't fall back in, won't be
famous southern singer,
hunger,
won't be
justice

A man shouted, "don't you talk."

hair breeze—night trembles

light through body

CLIP LIGHT

He's gone like desert,

like wet lands after the storm

—bristles from lights

brother singing needle

Sky's the limit

TEXAS YELLOW JACKET

won't you dance

brother

eyes rolled around his fists

spitting gold

dig a pit for him

father wrapped and left for dead

say this is my body

say this is just addiction

ally baby

his eyes two soft

oranges, he looks too thin to be your brother

rose petal tongue

we weren't supposed to leave without each other

watching your tongue rattle

like change in a cage of teeth

SAY ANYTHING

He's gone like desert

wetlands

after the storm

that can't grow

back not even with your used

Christmas trees

bristles from lights

singing needle

swapping tags,

       tag light

OVERDOSE

Messaging you dream boy
blurring that he's
gone and you're here
And you hear it all the time
Needle songs on hands
smell of morn
ings, you late
night, anything to hear
your name, and my
dreams are of celebrities
and men, dreaming
you back
years of needle
ends, prick my hand for you
carve you back
make my hand
against your cheek

TIDE

My head dizzy with pollen and the radio
cutting our bones away
face is tight
dreaming
his friends who disapproved

can't admit   to be right
And andy warhol looks great on white
museum of disco balls
big pink nothings

bodies almost taking new shapes
He's growing on me you whispered
rub your finger where that bright light
matched your eyes only brief
listening to shitty pop songs about how

 he could have just done more
maybe listened for once, made
a face in the window of the passing car,
held another type of dream,
your face

plastic making sky;
lines making a face
could have been a ghost
pretending to be a ghost
could have been you in my mouth again
pretending to be a ghost or a plow
floating, angelic
could have been a ghost
pretending to be a ghost

LIGHTSHEEN I.

I can't stop dreaming up a baby
not caring for another,
but body a vessel, nipples warm
tongue, breath, against my face,
stars for ships, grainy smudge of all nighters
anxiety of ripping film and quiet
of thoughts, words eating, dark room
blaring, "We are building a religion!"
I want to hold the sky
breathe rain, dream the tree back,
dream Rochelle back, roll her back
through Magnolia windows
breaking, brake ing press
curls to cheek, dashes to solid
line stay in one lane, how could we be any
where holding flowers, dipping
light, blowing out free
ways all free
dom, my body
dreaming french fries and king
cakes, night heart,
naked, swilling hand up her pink
shopping cart,
It's alright baby,
we are all sinners,
balling up hands for heart
beats, water in my house
black mold, it's all over
dark and stormy
eyes, humidity destroy
my heart belt, pool
light off boat bodies, honey
mud, my everything, can't turn it
down, corrupt little swamp
lids, try to move your toes
from your eye, it's all sliding
oil through sheets,
birds through mouth

RAIN HALO

childhood Red Rover, gripping hands trying to break the band, slide up and took head blood to the pavement, this drunk luck, love burning, the dying, bleeding out on concrete

keg to needles to all in pink, suburban dreams, cul de sac, the VHS hills, quiet of night, star dreams of a city, all the south clinging to the hot pavement

think you made it, in another kind of south, the kind of drips on guns, sun kick, the kind of bars all night, the perfect sling, run the river, underwater, underwhere, texas football, a kind of tribe, my homecoming, queen, candy wrappers, magnolias for hands, baby and waitress and her yes, flowers on lips, humidity your breath

flush it all and turn on the night, rain halo

DISSIPATION

Decadence of modern society. Looking
into your mouth. Portal. Sweetest scent.

Online longer than Vietnam. Longer
then the rat. The war of skin.

And media. Ring of sun against skin.
Predict our future babies. Palms
out as in prayer.

Palms out as in catching
rain. Drought all over
her face. The newest war.

REBIRTH

feel star on my knee
Mystery of birthing
upright
taught

someone else's
children
detached and close
all wrapped in one dialogue
of the body

wind pulling
stands
behind your ears
          messaging
someone new

KISS

little hands

America—

paint light

— burning out

blueberries turning palms

Allies turning secrets

river bodies—

The news keeps blasting his voice
Building walls
Make America

porch hot honey melon

watermelon in your teeth

wanting to kiss the patriarchy

out of that mouth

pulling clouds from the mud

blowing bubbles with

a rope and two sticks

be that home for me

BEAMING

What it means to have a gun, barrel
off the road, dead afternoon
light, glow
think myth, write it out,
praise that fake news,
rolling in a pit, I keep dreaming babies,
pressed to palms, belly
out and full, obsessed,
tons of kids pile into a bus,
full of something new

FLEDGELING

And someone plays a phone game in a cafe
shots bleating
in the afternoon
Still
like birds
escaping
scratches on the sky

SHOTS INTO DAY

Not sure how it happens
fit of night
sudden like dipping
concrete, night
slips over
hand, under
skirts, bags concrete
leaves on the side
of the road, young
boy run, his neighbor
shots cascading,
near his skull
too close for comfort,
news keeps ringing

become bird, become
sky, become
another boy
become a new
body, fitter, bullet
proof, night—
mare, air
unfolding

DEAR HEALTH INSPECTOR

Remove the crust from your eyelids
When's the last time before you knew?
climbing the light post
filling a gas can near the railroad
looking for pebbles against the skyline
everything becomes a haunting of your past
cars melting into morning
every business a facade for love-making
stealing beneath the table
holding hands together
holding them down
don't need to lie to me
you've seen them at their best
shiny stars between shiny noses
lost hands, holding hands
plates piled, mega millions for you
At the end of the day, you can't compare
every door frame a ghost of your other self
leaving a trail of receipts, wound up strings
dental floss, fishing wire, neck on a string
landline, landlocked,
every building on fire
pushing their eyes together
become unseen

STRIP MALL

For C.D. Wright

Bullet love

He told me his ammunition was expensive

Try firing a round
Metal through lips

Ring of Fire

Elvis love

Man waiting by the road with a walking stick
His fluorescent white and red hitting sky
He could have been Elvis
Accruing a crowd watching his every move
Or waiting for the right moment to be free

Freedom only Amazon could design
Birds have moved on already
Taking to space
Edge of the sun
Sitting on borrowed time

The bullets looked like a flock of birds he claimed

Bird love
And the bestsellers are about cities submerged
The bayou was at his toes
Wading and watching the clouds dip

specks of grey and sound
Flesh love
Beak love
One just crossed the street

Father like

Distinguished features
Sharp jawline

She rolled down her window to exclaim
"Something is dripping from your car, must be gas"
Drove off disappearing
back into the safety of objects and bright things

Basketball hoops and benches
Tight blue pillows soaking rays
Matching lawns, sprinklers
Hit rays, Cascade

No ones watering that grass
Machine love
No child is out on the corner

      Empty quarter bags
Loose hearts

The girl locked in his basement just down the street
 slipping into night
Television and the reemergence
men with candy coated eyes
With x marks the spot on her back
hands for tongues
Mass murder love

Her with chrysanthemums on both
shoulders faded
Scrunched, tight skin

sunken in
could have been my mother
sapphire, could have been Lima beans
full and round
Asking for some food,
I didn't have cash
Think of handing her my lunch

But pushing it back through my car window
Who carries cash anymore

FRITES

You couldn't hear
you were throwing french fries down my top

Blue horns
the mall scent

Foreign almost, artificial,
Like being in your mother's
apartment when she isn't there
Foreign objects

without delegated space
without her shadow
Her scent

Predictable
Heavenly

Almost another shade

Another self
Forming

Vulture perched eyelid

Closest to heaven she'll ever find

Swirling for the perfect kill

Assault weapons are on my mind

Again

Another bleeding mouth running the street

Making the front page

The new american dream

Palms as in prayer

CAROLE ANN BOONE

I lived without fear
       without a home

opaque
quiet
farm roads

I fell in love
with dying
in a car on top of a hill
wishing wells
 skipping stones
cutting class
Just your high school
Burnout

I'm no ordinary wo
man, just bagless
space
between home and church

between yes and a potential killer

love would be baptism
holy water spilling from
his mouth

body obliterated by faith
      by what the right thing to do is
was

charm
what my mother always wanted

Faith
idea of a proper

man

                falling for a killer
might have been a good man

avoid the dirt wash
           the ashy forehaads
taste of metal

my voice diminishing and his
becoming stately

oversized

everything but unreliable

SOME GIRLS AREN'T BORN THEY

push hoops through their skin, hair aflame
wedged between the sliding door and window
wedged between your jaw and upper lip
trapped between an open stretch of freeway
hand pressed thighs

push leaves through mouth
pretending to be a branch
become sharks. bitten fins trailing blood

Enemy, angelic
petrified, just trying to catch a break
lockets like constellations,
spritz liquor for perfume
open for strangers
anything for cash

dream

woman
blank as anchor blue blank
as glass blank this is crawling
in your mind this is your brother
high this is
dawn

hands, high on river
bend legs over couch
here he comes

leaving a face, make it blank
out black out, there he is babbling
out your eyes, there it is write, pull
the bike out, blank girl floating, blank
Rochelle rolling street, your mother, blank
night, blank its women falling,
sky, it's birth, ignite
hand, your mind this is your brother
sun this is dawn

HOPE CONFIGURATIONS

H-bomb hope

Haha half heart

so go with the flow baby

habitual hope

hack hope

Hail Mary, drink

your hands

hairnet, healers,

hop the train, half blue,
half life

jock strap,

               halo tease
hallucinate sweet

hoop something like   hope

MEMORY

sagging into morning; pull your hair; a faucet of fingers;
slammed together; sleep sliding; ocean; everyday wishing
for magic; pulling toes through sand; body through broken
glass; woman from sound; mirage; say her name

LAKE PONTCHARTRAIN

her name, spell

ocean, lake, mouth,

      flashback, her bike

floating in a river,

rolling, eyes

haunting for you,

drowning
metal frame

BEFORE DUSK

make a road map on the floor, her bike floating in the lake,
press your tongue to the back of your mouth, flood of you,
women rolling, bicycles and farmers market on the weekend,
televisions, stagnant water, hum, dawn, breaking, faces on
Good Morning America, flood of you, eyes and Amber alerts,
the moment before, how women fade into night,
undetectable, untraceable, unseen

NIGHT

Push the caterpillar off his shoulder, learn loss, swim through the fog of almost rain, the way the air burns crickets and silver, exhaust, exertion, exposed white roots of the purple flowers in her front yard. think love. think anything

ARTIFACTS

cup sliding between your eyes and mouth. liquid breath.
watching your eyes change shape. night eyes. haze of you.
chair thrown across the room. bending metal. out of shape.
cold against your skull. kitchen of your dreams. rounding
your spine. tell me. tell anyone. kitchen tile closest thing to
god

CODEPENDENCY

it all happened late, past midnight, flood of you, he takes his
cup and makes it your hand, filling and sliding, his hopes and
losses on the floor, his eyes change you, night, redemption,
mosquitoes creating wind, a chair becomes a mouth, a
simple tool, a possible weapon, a bent frame, you know this
is just moon gap, fireside, his escape, hand bends floor,
curve of your spine, make yourself into that chair, throw
yourself across the room, simple till the fall, and it's the
fragility of your body coming down, faith, mosquito creating
wind, holding on to things you taught yourself to love

WARNING SIGN

tulips in the park
sighing
magic
to be a liar
to have lied
oil in the gulf coast again

sticker in a dream
keeping me inside—
this is the patriarchy

pink paws under the tracks
tell me big Google
can't dream

to dream
dreaming him with no shirt
dreaming of having to hide the blood in the bathtub

tiny bodies waiting
often grey and unlovable
i meant unmovable
your voice a whisper i can't escape

ROADKILL

The police showing up and it's too familiar
The half clothed hide in the doorway
their uniforms turning into your blue
tiny bodies of water slide down your night

Your eyes tiny canopies
dark fleshy trees for mouth
Click the website and an ocean,
of sound, bird howls blast your monitor
feverishly clicking end
avoid disturbing my new you from sleep

I can't even remember what
we were arguing about
end of a new year
the freckle on my shoulder
another name for moon
your voice down my neck in rain

Dark fleshy trees for mouth
That night a canopy of kitchen utensils
Liquor around your eyes
tiny bodies of water slide down your night
Anyones night
Nightmare
Air unfolding

A tear rolling, a tear
body crumpled in a door frame
Or behind the closest closet
another entrance
Trying to become unseen

And you're brought back and staring at this officer
She keeps asking you, are you alright
Her eyebrows raised on a flight
Pierced lips, quiet, polite
The way his mouth moved in night
Your heart beating and thinking about mars
Something not so distant from here

ARTIFACTS II.

Plead for me

        Sigh
down my neck in rain

Can't be faith

        Just exist
In this body

        Years with one person

Begging for forgiveness

Birds

        screeching existence

Tired love soaked

Wings

Branches and rain

Wet pupils

Then the crash

Spring and rain

Plastic bag floating sky

Flag taking wind

MIGRANTLIGHT

I cannot feel my face anymore,

        memory rolling, burned

    our skin to sun

California shape, anything for body:

        typhoon, mackerel, pit,

this island : green, tongue, trash

    burning in heaps, can't

    be home

        mouths floating

    down the Mississippi,

the way bodies change in the sun,

        tongue slipped

        religious son,

I'm watching my hands

fade into another self,

bitter of the ocean

morning
two headlights colliding

becoming one

GREAT FLOOD

Wetness drag to the other side of this wet hell

method for cleaning up the oil

spill, again

the south spilling

into the sea,

desert far dream

everyone embodies water,

wet on her face, faces

floating on the harbor

too far to notice any resemblance to your brother

faces blurring into one gold frame

your hands

soaked in dew

faces pulling closer to shore

all piled on top of each other

awe struck at someone who resembles you

caught in some similarities

MOUTHING MOUNTAIN

A woman clipping
nails on the subway
A man quickly
putting his feet into rubber
boots Banded
together like beach spots

rush hour mist
bag pulled high
subway shoulder
the way we move through water
Who are the real Buddhists?
The violence of a sign the moment
before you go
above ground.

Every receipt has a lottery number. My friend collects
them in her wallet,
makes a pillow,
catch her dreams.
A man said he won
once. It could take your whole
life. Why
ever leave?

BLUE NUDE

I wear my hair in two braids
pinned back. Trying to hide

every characteristic. I made
my body out in the window sill. Tired

corner of my room I shared with my sister
Desperate for bones. Singing skin songs.

Tightness. I pushed every stuffed toy around me
when I slept to feel a soft brush against my shoulder

Something like credibility. Magnets.
Two forces inevitably pulling towards

each other. Pushing back.
Handwritten slips of paper
from a boy wanting a body that he sees.

wanted to write back wondering what body
he was writing about. Eyes

fighting for flight. Sexualized before I could
even notice you. The internet twisting

my wrist again. Bird,
 bunny, anything for body

SPIGOT

In the shower, I become a fountain
mouth spitting water

Shower head dripping

against tile

waiting for water to get warm
cool on your neck

knowing I left

washing a small wing down the drain

flood of you

A series of heartbreaks
consecutive, fleeting
flood of you

Speaking from my offices offices orifices
Why isn't that a word for opening ?

A loud comment
something dark
pressing my fingers deep
soft flesh moving
hands to higher places
wanting to be touched

FAVORITE EX

She mentioned that he is her
favorite from bars or group therapy
back porches, bank entrances,
grocery lines, hospital curtains
tell me about your past lovers
lazy and senile
repressed and emotional
the drunk and abusive ones
listening to men
coordinate for an event out
side your local coffee shop
break your mouth again
but your distracted from this reality
the most restrictive abortion law in history
familiar faces at a restaurant
could she be your favorite ex
painting your face on a piece of wood
just red, blue and black
telling where her favorite dumpsters are
her self portraits become her cheering squad
imagine brushing her hair over your mouth
strands slip between your teeth
familiar faces at a restaurant
falling in love with just
their features
features in silence

I-10 W

I keep seeing all these dead
animals on the road
Evacuation routes   light pierces clouds
not directly but in beams
Its raining with the sun out   wonder
what you could be doing now

Self, Seigun

deer couldn't wander this far you think
there are no trees for them   hide in how could they
be out this far with only sun

flowers to hide   burnt grass for skin
Asphalt melt
tuna melt another name for self
Like skin   shredded pebbles

Nothing little about hay barrels
Hay bodies

                Fast food utopia
                Burgers for hands

Just want to find a place to sleep in this field

Want to feel

They put crawfish traps in rice fields
Say this is killing two birds with one stone
Say we have to do what
we can to survive

SOFT BEGINNINGS

hardly looking in each others eyes
fire, metaphor for prayer
calling you, everything
turn, become that obsession
moving me to hands on your chest
pull around you
messaging, finding ourselves
swimming pool, your body of water
pull my leg closer, slipped
 beneath the surface,
hair pulled, soft beginnings
imagine you sleeping
nothing,
everything,
pulled your car into park,
headlights softening
your silhouette into night

SOFT BEGINNINGS

saw the meme about Edgar Allan Poe / cellars / birds on
your chest / I'm becoming obsessed / trying to have as little
as possible / bodies occupying space / lose a tooth / heart
underwater again / I used to collect my teeth in a small silver
tin / trying to hold on to something / body / decompose /
wanting to press them back into your mouth / chewing gum /
fruity flavor / the one with the smiling zebra on the package /
silver flecks on your thumb / snapchat / caged body / blue /
mouth / desire / nude / pictures on the tiny light in your
pocket / subtleties / mirror reflecting / hair around your areola
/ wrinkles on your neck / birthmark in fluorescent light /
sudden shadow of your jaw

LIGHTSHEEN

I'm begging for rain

Holding a pocket
          open wide

Hungry mouth
children with plastic bags

Their eyes gleaming with your brother

Ode to you in the dark   just an old name from the
                                                  past

Pushing war to the back of your mouth

War an elaborate metaphor for puberty
War was shopping for the essentials,

 buying clothing from target,
anything that could fit

brushing

truth

everything

anything

because chaos

details

Good Price

Good Price

another

possible

salvation

light　　　　hinges

Additional Acknowledgments

Many special thanks to my mentors Joseph Lease and Donna de la Perrière for your fierce love and inspiration to find my voice and follow it

Many thanks to all of the faculty and peers at CCA for your close reads, compassion, and loyalty: Chloe, Colin, Natalie, Samiat, Rachel, Melissa, Veronica, Vanessa, Zack, Ben, Patrick Nelson, Kate, Charlie, Allie, Andrew, Berenice

Special thanks to Taipei Poetry Collective: Sandee, Ashley, Leora, Ariana, Shameez, Kira, Jonathan for being a place to grow, create and share

For being my muse, crafter, and life of the party: Mathew

Special thanks to the people who shaped me: Clélie, Hope, Valerie, Hayley, Liza, Sara, Kayla, Kota, KC, Dominique, Virginia, Mandy, Lisa, Erin, Vicky, Nicole, John, Shanda, Kayln, Steffy, Davielle, Roem, Amber, Arlo, Adeline, Aunt Liz, Aunt Victoria, Dave, Fran, Dear Dear

For the Chaus: Constance, Wakin and Andrew for helping me find a home and walking with it

For my family: Tim, Suzanne, Jeannette, Donovan, Dorothy, Kelli, Suzanne, Michelle, David, GG, Gran, Sue, and Coco

Born at the foot of the Alamo and raised in New Orleans, **Alexandra** earned her MFA in Creative Writing from California College of the Arts. She is the author of chapbook, *Femmesturary* dancing girl press, 2016. Find her work at *Second Stutter, In Parentheses Magazine, LIT,* and *Aspasiology* in response to Donna de la Perrière. On her three year hiatus teaching English in Taipei, Taiwan, she co-hosted Taipei Poetry Collective, a reading series and workshop. Find some of her photography at *Gravel Magazine* and Instagram @poetsforsound

www.ingramcontent.com/pod-product-compliance
Lightning Source LLC
Chambersburg PA
CBHW021156090426
42740CB00008B/1113